HOLY
REVELATION

I Am The Lord

HOLY REVELATION

I Am The Lord

TAYLOR RUSSEL STONE

ARPress
ILLUMINATING IDEAS
EMPOWERING VOICES

ARPress
45 Dan Road Suite 5
Canton, MA 02021

Hotline: 1(888) 821-0229
Fax: 1(508) 545-7580

Ordering Information:

Quantity sales. Special discounts are available on quantity purchases by corporations, associations, and others. For details, contact the publisher at the address above.

Printed in the United States of America.

ISBN-13:	Softcover	979-8-89356-135-7
	eBook	979-8-89356-137-1
	Hardback	979-8-89356-136-4

Library of Congress Control Number: 2024912049

Permute: To change the order, arrangement such as numbers of letters.

In Revelation of the Holy Bible, five statements were said, which allow the people to identify the LORD.

I am...
First and Last
The beginning and the end
The bright and the morning star
The Root and offspring of David
Alpha and Omega

Prelude: G O D
          7 6 4
           17
          L o v e
          3 6 4 5
           18
GOD/LOVE: 35: C R E A T O R
  17   18   3 9 5 1 2 6 9

CONTENTS

INTRODUCTION

The mystics of Judaism and the Rebbes of the Kabbalah believed the alphabet of the Holy Creation, Hebrew, contained numerical values. The book herein written contains the encoded values of the various personifications of the Tree of Life, found in the end-time English Alphabet.

> To find the one (1) : 1
> Incarnated under human numbers (1-9) : 9
> You use the English alphabet (26) : 8 (1944)

The Lord hid his face from the chosen, and in keeping with that fact, in many cases you have to permute the word values to arrive at the divine manifestation. The task at hand to present Immanu-el (God with us), the creator, etc., and make the specifics verifiable. This book is a journey and the end is the realization of God's human/Divine identity.

ENGLISH END-TIME DECRYPTION TABLE

1	2	3	4	5	6	7	8	9	To check the value of the word:
A	B	C	D	E	F	G	H	I	V E R I F Y
J	K	L	M	N	O	P	Q	R	459967
S	T	U	V	W	X	Y	Z		40

v

I am...
    First and Last
    S T O N E
    1   FIVE
  ONE   6 5
6 5
  22: L O R D
    3 6 9 4

TAYLOR RUSSELL STONE
    28   2 5   19 : 72 : 9
5, 4 1944   27 : 9
4                $\frac{4}{22}$

Social S.N. = 5, 3 1944
Birth date = 5, 4 1944
      17 / 18: 35 : CREATOR

  I am ...
    First and Last $9\,^{\text{NINE}}_{5\ \ 5}$ 10

                      $9\,^{\text{NINE}}_{5\ \ 5}$ 10

                      $4\,^{\text{FOUR}}_{6\ \ 9}$ $\frac{15}{35 : \text{CREATOR}}$

                             35

PART I

In this PART the number 77 will be the number of INTEREST, The Supreme Being, The Father of Heaven AND the Prince of Peace all have sums for their letter values which equal 77. when using the first and last criteria for Mr. Stone's NAME you arrive at 77. The first Letter of Taylor is T which is two (256) or thirteen and the last letter is NINE (5955) or 24, Added together they equal 37. The first and last of the letters of stone are 1 (ONE) 655 or 16 and Five (6945) or 24. added together you obtain 40. When 37 and 40 are combined you get 77. Using the first name and the birth year arrive *also* at 77, *If* A=B and B = A th*en* A is *B* an*d* B is A

        I am . . . First AND Last
            TAYLOR RUSSELL STONE   7̱2
            5,4, 1944   2̱7
                    77   99

        The Supreme Being
        15   34   28
                77

The Prince of Peace
15   38   3   21
77

I am . . . First AND Last
The Supreme Being
2 5   1   5 2   7
7   6   9

22 : LORD
The Prince of Peace / LORD
77   22

King of kings, and LORD of Lords
2957 3 29571 1   22   3   23 : 99

The Father of Heaven
15   31   3   28   : 77

THE ANOINTED ONE
15   37   16
68 :   77
Permute + 1 – 1

The Chosen One
15   28   16
59 : 77
Permute + 2 – 2

The Covenant of the Lord
15   31   3   6   22
77

2

The Holy ONE of Israel
6   24   16   3   28
        77

Everlasting GOD
        51   17
            68
Permute +1 −1 : 77

All-Knowing Father
7   39   31
        77

The Presence of the Lord
6   40   3   6   22
        77

The Lord GOD almighty
15   22   17   41
        95 : 77
Permute − 2+2

Space   17
17135
Time   20
2945
Continuum   40
365295334   77: THE PRINCE of Peace
                    15   38   3   21

612859   /
FATHER   /   Creator of All Things
31   /   35   3   7   32
                    77

3

31 + 77 : 108 :   99 : king of kings, AND LORD of Lords
  Permute – 1+1
      Crucifixion
      39339696965
      95 : 77
Permute –2+2
      The Crown of Creation
        6   28   3   40
          77

      The master of the Continuum
        6   22 3 6   40
          77

      The Covenant of spirit
        6   31   3 37
          77

      the Vengeance of the Lord
      6   40   3 6 22
          77

      the ONCE AND FUTURE king
      6   19   1   28   23
          77

      the Royal MONARCH
      15 26   36
          77

        Omnipotent God
         51   17
          68 : 77
        Permute +1-1

The Revelation of the Lord
15   49   3 6   22
95 : 77
Permute −2+2

The Judge of MANKIND
15   20   3   30
68 : 77
Permute +1-1

The Awakened One
15   28   16
59 : 77
Permute +2-2

The King Eternal
15   23   30
68 : 77
Permute +1-1

I am The Lord God
9 5 15   22   17
68 : 77
Permute +1-1

The Knowledge of God
15   42   3 17
77

Holy , Holy , Holy is the Lord of Hosts
6   6   6 10 6   22 3   18
77

5

Cherisher and Sustainer of the Worlds

    57   1   36   3 6   28

Permute 131 │ 77

    -6+6 │

Lord of the Worlds

   22   3 6   28

       59 : 77

Permute +2-2

Immanent/Manifest

    35   33

     68 : 77

Permute +1-1

Unified Field

    41   27

    68 : 77

Permute +1-1

The Lords might

   15   23   30

     68 : 77

Permute +1-1

The Hari Krishna : 77 : The Incarnate Lord

15 27   35   15   40   22

I am . . .

First and Last

The Lord

2 5 3 4 : 77

The Prince of Peace : 34 / Immanu-el   7
2 5 7   5 3 7   5

The Everlasting Father : 34 | Immanu-el $\frac{7}{77}$
 2 5 5   7 6   9

First and Last

TAYLOR RUSSELL STONE   72
5,4,1944   27

Name Sum   Seventy-Two
           1   6   7
                                      : 77
Birthday Sum   Twenty-Seven   7
              2   5
       Savior of the Multitude
      33 3 6   35
           77

The Harmony of the Lord
  6   40 3 6 22
        77

Indivisible One
  52   16
    68 : 77
Permute + 1-1

The Perfect One
  15 37   16
   68 : 77
Permute +1-1

Sovereign Lord Protector
51/6   4   49
59 : 77
Permute + 2-2

A Stone for Stumbling
1 19 21   36
77

Master of Ceremonies
22 3   52
77

The Seat of Power
15 9 3 32
59
$\left. \vphantom{\begin{matrix}59\\2\text{-}2\end{matrix}} \right|$: 77
Permute   + 2-2

High Command
32   27
59 : 77
+ 2 - 2

O Lord, our Lord
6 22 9 22
59 : 77
Permute + 2-2

My Lord, our God
11 22 9 17
59 : 77
Permute +2-2

8

The Pinnacle of Perfection

6   38   3   57

$\dfrac{104}{-3+3}$: 77

Permute

Righteousness Seed

62   15

77

Holy of Holies

24   3   32

$\dfrac{59}{2\text{-}2}$: 77

Permute   +

Rock of offence

20   3   36

59 : 77

Permute +2-2

PART II

THE ROCK OF ISRAEL

15   20 3   28

66

I am

First and Last

9   NINE

5   5

Five   Five

6   5

TAYLOR RUSSELL STONE

28/1	25/7	1/18	
9	9	9	
11	11	11	33

5,4,1944

9 9 9

11 11 11   33

66

PSALMS . . . Our Fortress

18   39

$\frac{57}{}$: 66

Permute + 1-1

The Holy Child
15   24   27
66

THE Messenger
15   42
57 : 66
Permute + 1-1

THE Everlasting
15   51
66

My Redeemer
11   46
57 : 66
Permute +1-1
His Loving Kindness
18   66
84 : 66
Permute +2-2

Chosen of the Faithful
28   3   6   38
75 : 66
Permute −1+1

My Covenant of Peace
11   31   3   21
66

The Sovereign
15   51
66

TENDER Mercies
30   36
66

My Light and My Salvation
11   29   1   11   32
84 : 66
Permute –2+2

The beauty of the Lord
15   20   3 6   22
66

Holy Solemnity
24   42
66

Note :

First and Last 77   SEVEN SEVEN : 66
1   5 1   5

A Singularity
1   56
57
: 66
Permute   +1-1

The Heavenly Father
15   38   31
84
: 66
Permute – 2+2

DIVINE INTERVENTION
       36   66
           102
          ――― : 66
Permute −4+4

GOD'S Eternal LOVE
    18   30   18
            66

Holy PERSON
   24   33
       57 : 66
Permute +1-1

Strong TOWER
   30   27
   57 ⎤
       ⎥ : 66
Permute +1-1 ⎦

The LIVING Waters
    6   37   23
            66

The Lord GOD of Hosts
   6   4   17   3   18
          48 : 66
Permute +2-2

Lord of the Throne
   22   3   6   35
           66

13

The Holy Morning
6   24   45
$$75 : 66$$
Permute – 1+1

DIVINE PROVIDENCE
$$93 : 66$$
Permute – 3+3

The SEVENTH SON
15   30   12
$$57 : 66$$
Permute + 1-1

WhirlWIND
$$57 : 66$$
Permute + 1-1

The Well of Salvation
15   16 3   32
66

Kingdom of God
37   3   17
57 : 66
Permute +1-1

The glorious Majesty of the Lord
6   44/8   21   3 6   22
66

The Root and offspring of David

6   23   10   56   3   22

$$\frac{120}{\text{Permute} - 6+6} : 66$$

The Merciful

15   42

$$\frac{57}{+1-1} : 66$$

Lord Krishna   .

22   35

$$\frac{57}{\text{Permute} + 1-1} : 66$$

King of the EARTH

23   3   6   25

$$\frac{57}{\text{Permute} + 1-1} : 66$$

The Mighty ONE of Jacob

6   37/1   16   3   13

$$\frac{39}{+3-3} : 66$$

the God of Gods, and LORD of Lords

6   17 3 18   10   22   3   23

$$\frac{102}{\text{Permute} - 4+4} : 66$$

The Throne of DAVID

6   35   3   22

66

PART III

JEHOVAH / the LION of ISRAEL
1586418   6   23   3   28
33   60

I Am
    First AND Last
    TAYLOR RUSSELL STONE   72   9
    5,4,1944   27   9
    Birthday 4   4
another way

	NINE			
	5	5		
Five	6	5	9	11
	NINE			
	5	5	9	11
	6	5		
	four			
	6	5		11
				33

First AND Last   Creator
               3   9   krishna
    Allah   33   2   1
    1   8
          Elohim
          5   4

I Am . . .
    First AND Last
ANOTHERWAY   Taylor R. Stone
                    1 7 19
   NINE   9 9 9   30
   5   5   10 10 10
                    5, 4, 1944
                    9 9 9
                    10 10 10   30
                                60

          The Path
          15 18
            33
          VICTOR
            33   :   The Victor
                    15 33
                      48
                         : 66
         Permute   + 2-2

PSALMS . . . a sun and a SHIELD
          1 9   10 1   30
            51
               : 33
   Permute −2+2

" . . . I will raise . . ."
    STANDARD
          27   5,4,1944
                    9 9 9
                    11 11 11 : 33
                    2 2 2
                    Aquarius
   His Justice
     9   24
      33

Day of Judgement
12 3   36
        51 │ : 33
Permute -2+2 │

DIVINE JUSTICE
36   24
60

The Lion of Israel   60 : 33
                    -3+3
Immutable
33
Immutable Law
33   9
42 : 33
Permute − 1+1

The Nature of God
6   25 3 17
    51 : 33
  -2+2

Praise the Lord
5   6   22
33

The Ultimate One
15   29   16 : 60
6   11   16 : 33
                   93

93 : 66 The Rock of Israel
Permute −3+3

God Supreme
17   34
        51 : 33
Permute –2+2

The Potter's Touch
6   32   22
        60 : 33
Permute –3+3

The Grace of God
6   25 3 17
        51 : 33
Permute –2+2

Words of Power
25   3   32
        60 : 33
Permute –3+3

The Emperor
15   45
        60 : 33
Permute –3+3

An Anomaly
15   27
6   27
        33

The Wise One
6   20   16
        42 : 33
Permute -1+1

YHVH Tzavoat : LORD of Hosts

$$27 \qquad 24$$

$$51 : 33$$

Permute −2+2

All-Powerful

$$7 \qquad 44$$

$$51 : 33$$

Permute −2+2

The DEITY

$$6 \qquad 27$$

$$33$$

The Arm of the LORD

$$15 \quad 14 \ 3 \ 6 \quad 22$$

$$60 : 33$$

Permute −3+3

I Am. . .

First AND Last

First AND Last

6	2	8

The beginning and the END   6

2   4

The bright and morning STAR   11

2   9

The Root and offspring of DAVID   6

2   4

Alpha and Omega

1   1   2

$$33$$

GOD of Jacob

$$17 \ 3 \quad 13$$

$$33$$

PART IV

EL, Almighty GOD
53

PSALMS... My Defence
11   33
44 : 53
Permute +1-1

Righteousness
62 : 53
Permute −1+1

The Love of GOD
15   18   3   17
53

TAYLOR'S SSN Summed
44 : 53
Permute +1-1

The LORD'S Truth
15   23   24
62 : 53
Permute −1+1

The most High and Mighty
6   4   32   1   37/1
          44 : 53
Permute +1-1

The Big Kahuna
6 18   20
       44 : 53
Permute +1-1

Holy, Holy, Holy. Lord God Almighty
6   6   6   4   17   5
          44 : 53
Permute +1-1

Wrath of the Lamb
25 3 6   10
       44 : 53
Permute +1-1

The Lord on high
6   22 11 5
       44 : 53
Permute +1-1

A Peaceable Ruler
1   32   29
       62 : 53
Permute −1+1

I Am. . .
   First AND Last
      First AND Last
        27   10   7   44 : 53
           Permute +1-1

   Alpha and Omega
     20 1   23   44 : 53
        Permute +1-1

5,3, 1944   26
5,4 1944   27
             53

          Powerful
          44 : 53
      Permute +1-1

        Paragon of Virtue
          36   3   32
           71 : 53
      Permute –2+2

I Am . . .
First And Last
        Wonderful   8
        5   3
        Counselor   12
        3   9
        The Mighty God   6
        2   4
     The Everlasting FATHER 11
   2   9
    The Prince of Peace   7
   2   5   44

$^{44}:$ 53 EL
+1 -1

The Enlightment
6   65
$^{71}:$ 53
Permute −2+2
Permute TORAH
26 9 1 8
5,3, 1944
MADHI   5,3, 1944
EL MUSTAFA   5,3, 1944

5,3, 1944 | 3645
EL   LOVE

First and last of Mr. Stone's birthmonth and last name render
80 which permutes to 53, EL. First and last of his birthmonth
and birthyear also yield 80 permuting to 53, EL.

PART V

El SHADDAI
5   NINE   55
         5

SHADDAI
1814419 : 28

The Lord's Favor
15   23   26
      64 : 55
Permute −1+1

Unfathomable
46 : 55
Permute +1-1

The DIVINE Presence
15   36   40
        91 : 55
Permute −4+4

Ramachandra
46 : 55
Permute +1-1

Holy Night
24   31

Almighty LIVING God/SHADDAI
28

Allah, the Merciful
16   6   42
$64 : 55$
Permute −1+1

Alpha and Omega's kingdom come
20   1   24   37   9
$91 : 55$
Permute −4+4

The Creator of the Universe
6   35   3 6   41
$91 : 55$
Permute −4+4

TAYLOR : 28 : Shaddai :
217369   1814419

ANAgram TAYLOR : Royal T

The Comfort of the Lord
6   36   3 6   22
$73 : 55$
Permute −2+2

Beautiful SON
34   12
$46 : 55$
Permute +1-1

I AM . . .
   First and Last

NAMED SUMMED   9 NINE
     FIVE FIVE   11
     6   5

Birthdate summed   9 NINE
     FIVE FIVE
     6   5   11
Birthday   4 Four
       Six   Five   6
       1   5   28

   The Lord
    6   22 : 28
   Tzaddi
   281449 : 28

         The off-forgiving
          6 14   62
            82 : 55
      PERMUTE –3+3

The HAND of the LORD
  6   13   3 6   22
      55

   The king of Jerusalem
   15   23 3   32

73 : 55

-2+2

CROWN

28

AN ENIGMA

15/6   31

37 : 55

Permute + 2-2

ETERNAL ONE

30   16

46 : 55

PERMUTE +1-1

The Voice of the LORD

15   27 3 6   22

73 : 55

Permute –2+2

OMNISCIENCE

55

My Deliverer

11   53

64 : 55

Permute –1+1

I Am . . .

First AND Last

The INCARNATE Lord

2 5 9   5 3 4

28

INTERCESSOR

55

Maher Shalal Hash Baz

	27		17		18	11
+1	GOD			-1		
	28				28	

SHADDAI   TAYLOR

Maher Shalal Hash Baz

27	17	18	11
-3	8		-5
24	25		24

The living God RUSSELL   The Mighty God

Maher Shalal Hash Baz

	27	17	18	11
+10	17		-10	
37	GOD		19	

Spirit   STONE

PART VI

The EVERLASTING FATHER
6   51   31
88

LORD of Hosts
22 3 18 : 43

Isaiah
   Chapter 8
I Am . . .
     First AND Last
Maher Shalal Hash Baz
4   9 1   3 8 8 2 8
     43
I am . . .
   First AND Last
           5 3, 1944
           5 4, 1944

     May Three
     4 7 2 5   18
     May Four
     4 7 6 9   26 : 44
2)   May Third
     4 7 2 4   17
     May Fourth
     4 7 6 8   25 : 42

3) May Three
    4 7 2 5   18
    May Fourth
    4 7 6 9   25 : 43
4) May Third
    4 7 2 4   17
    May Four
    4 7 6 9   26 : 43

PERMUTE 44 42 : 4 3 43 43 43
             -1 +1   7 7 7 7
                            28 / TAYLOR/SHADDAI
         43 : Lord of Hosts

        The Everlasting Lord
         15   51   22
                 88

        The Secret of his TABERNACLE
         15   25   3 9   36
                 88

            The Spirit of Truth
             15   37 3 24
                     79 │ : 88
        PERMUTE +1-1   │
I am . . .
        First AND Last
        First AND Last
         27   10   7   44
        . . . Alpha and Omega
          20   1   23   44
                                 88

                    31

wholesome
43
The Way Everlasting
15 13   51
79 : 88
PERMUTE +1-1

TERRIBLE Presence OF THE LORD
44   40   3   6   22
115 : 88
PERMUTE –3+3

Thy ROD and Thy Staff
17   19   10   17   16
79 : 88
PERMUTE +1-1

My KINDNESS
11   32
43

The Rock of Salvation
15   20   3   32
70 : 43
PERMUTE –3+3

Your WINGS
25   27
52 : 43
-1+1

A Righteous Branch
1   50   28
79 : 88
PERMUTE +1-1

32

I Am . . .
  First AND Last
    LORD of Hosts
    3 4 3 8 1
      STONE
        19

TAURUS / STONE
213931 / 12655

King of Kings, AND LORD of LORDS
  5-4, 1944 – TAYLOR RUSSELL STONE
  27   28   25   19
  72
  9   9
            99
    The Right HAND of the LORD
    15   35   18   3 6   22
                  99

    5-4, 1944
     9   9 9   27
  NINE   NINE NINE
  5955   5955 5955
    24   24   24   72 : TAYLOR RUSSELL STONE
                            28   25   19
                  99

  The LORD, OUR Righteousness
  15   22   18   62
          117 : 99
          -2+2
I Am . . .
  First AND Last

34

WONDERFUL
5   3   8

COUNSELLOR
3   9   12

The MIGHTY GOD
2 5 4   7 7 4   29

The EVERlasting FATHER
2 5 5   7 6   9   34

The Prince of Peace
2 5 7 5 3 7 5   <u>34</u>
                           117
            117 : 99

  PERMUTE –2+2
    The Tree of the Knowledge of Evil and GOOD
     6   21 3 6   42   3 21 1   23
                  126 : 99
                  -3+3

PART VII

CREATOR
35
The Creator
15   35
    50
OUR SALVATION
18   32
    50
The ROAD
15   20
    35
Reign
35

Triumphant
    50
5-3, 1994
5-4, 1944
17 / 18 : 35
Evil/GOOD
21   23
    AND
    10

54: THE LORD GOD
REVERENCE
50

I am . . .
First AND Last   FIRST
                27   27
            OMEGA
              23   <u>23</u>
                            50

The Balance
15   20
   35
A Buddha Field
1   22   27
   50
     Dhammapada
   35
       The king of Love
6 23 3 18
   50

PSALMS:
My Strength
11   39
   50
Righteous
   50
Refuge
   35
7th Imam
17, 1944
   35

37

PART VIII

CORRESPONDENCES

The Blessed Holy ONE

    6   3   6   16

31

FATHER

31

I Am . . .

  First AND Last

  TAYLOR R. STONE

  2   5

5-4, 1944

24, 25, 55, 54 : 158

68 : 77 The Prince of Peace

    Permute +1-1

Omnipotent	51
Omnipresent	58
Omniscient	49
	158
	68 : 77
	+1-1

I Am . . .

  First AND Last

ISAIAH 28
          . . . A Stone   15
             1   5
         A tried stone   15
         1   5

A precious cornerstone   15
1   5
A sure foundation   <u>15</u>
1   5
                     60: the lion of Israel
                       6   23 3   28

Birthday 4
       four
       6639   24
       6 9   <u>15</u>
             39 : 66 the Rock of Israel
                 15   20 3   28

       TAYLOR R. STONE
        2
    5-4, 1944 : 24
        4

The Living GOD
   6   1   17 : 24

The Mighty GOD
   6   1   17 : 24

       Holy
       24

NINE
24
Truth
24
Pure
24
Equivalencies
I Am . . .
FIRST AND Last
Joshua
1   1
TAYLOR STONE
28   19
1   1
Alpha and Omega
1   1
TAYLOR RUSSELL STONE
2   9 9 12 3 1   5
11   3   6
20
Joshua
20
TAYLOR
2   9
Light
29
TAYLOR
yo al
76 13
17:GOD

PART IX

The Adversary
      6   41
47
         11
      JESUS
11
Adam AND Eve
   10   1   14
         16/7
MAN AND MEN
   10   1   14
         16/7
Jesus Christ
      11   32
       2   5 : 7
      Devil
      45493
       25 : 7
      Vatican
       25/7
      YESHUA
      751831
         25
7

ENCODED BEFORE Time
First AND Last
ONE WAY   YESHUA Josephus
               7   1 1   1
                        10 : SATAN
                               11215

ANOTHER WAY:
    7+1+71+1+1+1+1+1 =20
    Death =20
    45128
    Jesus Christ
    1   1 3   2
    1+1+1+2+3+2+3+1
            14
            EVE
            14
Satan and Jesus Christ / Lucifer
      10   1   14   38
      25   11 : JESUS
      7
    Adam and Eve
       10   1 14
    25
    7
  SERPENT
  1597552 : 34 : Mother
  7   462859
Evil/Pagan : 21 : Mary
    5493 71715   3   4197

    -----

    10 : SATAN
    1st AND last

42

The Abomination of Desolation

2 5 1   5 3 4   5
   7   6   3   9
        25 : 7

              Jesus Christ
              11   32 : 25
              Pagan Faith
               21   26
                   47
                  11 : JESUS
                     15131

PART X

SINCE this Chapter originally had to do with subject matter which had Nothing to do with establishing the Lord's identity it has been deleted.

Summation

Permute following
>   Torah
>   26918 : 5-3, 1944
>   FAITH
>   61928 : 5-3, 1944
>   Hope
>   8675 : 5-3, 1944
>   Train
>   29195 : 5-3, 1944

The Book of Creation orally transmitted and attributed to the Patrarch Abraham concerns the characteristics of God. The key to determining Immanu-el's birthday is found in the statement:

In the beginning is embedded the end, and in the end is found the beginning.

IMMANU-EL

944153-53

In the beginning 9 is embedded one
and in the end one is found the beginning

1944 53—53
53-53, 1944 or 8-8, 1944
or 8 Iyar = 8-8, 1944
ON May 4th, 1944 the day in the Jewish Calendar
was 8 Iyar.

The Spirit of God joined the Holy Vessel

ON 5-3, 1944 and the Creator, Immanu-el was born
At 7:16AM ON 5-4, 1944
Right Side: TAYLOR is Immanu-el *

	28	10	34	72		
			34		34	

LEFT SIDE: TAYLOR'S Lord of Hosts

	29		43	_72_		
			43			
				144	_43_	
					77	

77 : The Prince of Peace
*Revelation: Chapter 2 Verse 17
I Am . . .
First and Last
Alef-ty   TAU-RUS

5   3 , 1944
May   Third, 1944
12   32
3   5 or
5 3
3 5 , 1944
on 5–3, 1944 the Spirit of the

LORD attached to the Holy Vessel and
ON 5–4, 1944 at 7:16 Am Immanu-el
was born. 5-4, 1944 is 8 Iyar on the
Hebrew Calendar.
Immanu-el : 5 3 5-3, 1944
    8–Iyar
      9719 or 8-8, 1944
5 3 – 5 3, 1944

      Alpha and Omega
     20   1   23
        44
Mr. Stone's Social Security number summed: 44

Crucifixion of the Lord of Hosts
1973 to 1994 : 21 years
    365 days
    x21
    ————
    7665 days
    x24 hours
    ————
    183960 hours
     999 O – Omega
5-4, 1944
9   99 : the Lord God
    Cross cut on Tree of Life's back IN culmination
  of crucifixion spiritual Love.
       Occult : Hidden
    To he who has understanding:
      May Four
      4 7 6 9
        26 : 5-3, 1944

Scale of Justice
Russell : 25/7   7 Numerology number for Justice
TAYLOR/HEAVEN   Hell/Stone
        28   19
         1   1
          By your Acts you are judged.

I Am . . .
 First AND Last
        Je'hovah   33   Three Three
                             2   5 2   5
                                 77

The Prince of Peace   77

                             Seven Seven
                             1   5 1   5
                                 66

The Rock of Israel   66

                          Six Six
                          1 6 1 6
                             77

The Supreme Being   77
LORD   22 Two Two
                         2 6 2 6
                            88

The Everlasting Father   88
                             Eight Eight
                             5   2 5   2
                                 77

   The Christos
        15   39 : 54 The Lord God
               Zeus
               8531 or 54,44

47

Horus
86931 : 5-4, 1944
ZION
8965
28/ shaddaI/ TAYLOR

ZERO
8596
28 : SHADDAI/TAYLOR
From Nothing (ZERO) everything came
   Mr. Stone's SSN Ending : 5777 or 5-3, 1944
   ADONAI
      26 or 5-3, 1944
The Lamb of God
 6   10 3 17
36/EL Shaddai
 God/ the Lord
  17   6 22
      45/ Most High
   13 32
Abraham 26/8
ISAAC   15/6
JACOB   13/4

18: 1944
25 3 17
    Wrath of God
 7 3 8 = 18 : 1944
I am . . .
First AND last
 1944
    ONE FOUR
    6 5 6 9
  26 : 5-3, 1944

The first and last of God and love equal
    God and Love
Kabbalah
    Ehyeh 33
    Asher 24
    Ehyeh 33 : 90
      -5+5
     _____

    45 : Most High
  13   32

Imma
  18   53- 53, 1944 YAH/Allah
  18   34   16

DIN
  18 : 1944   5-3, 1944

          Adonai
          26/5-3, 1944

        I, the Lord am AN
           Avatar
           1944

Holy Bible
        Lev, Chap. 26 verse 12
        Zech. Chap. 2 verses 10 AND 11

I am . . .
Alpha AND Omega
The Rock of Israel
LORD, Creator
  22   35
     57 : 66
   +1-1

I am . . .
The bright and Morning Star
    There are five Morning Stars:
    Mercury, Venus, Mars, Saturn AND Jupiter
At 7:16 Am on 5-4, 1994 Jupiter was the Morning Star
The Church of Satan changed the original NAME of the Zodiac
May to Venus to imply the Creator was Satan.
In May in the Northern Hemisphere Venus is the Evening STAR,
        Jupiter
        36 : El Shaddai
         66
        six six
        1 6 1 6
         77
        I am . . .
         First AND last
        Redeemer
        9   9
          99: king of kings, AND LORD of Lords
        Mister   Taylor Stone
         30   28   19   : 77
        Hashem Adonai
         27   26
        5-4, 1944 5-3,1944

PART XI

What information can be derived from the birthday of Mr.
Stone, Let us see

    5-4, 1944

Five   Four,   1944

6945 6639   99

 24   24   NINE NINE

  6   6 Five Five Five Five

         6 5   6 5

              22   22 : LORD

   66 : The Rock of Israel

66 + 22 = 88 : The Everlasting Father

    66

   six six

  1 6 1 6 : 77 : The Prince of Peace

      77+22 : 99 : king of kings, AND LORD of Lords

  The ONE : 31 : FATHER

   15   16

  Great Spirit

  79512/6 37 : 43 : LORD of Hosts

I am . . .

    First AND last

TAYLOR R. STONE

2   5 : 7

I Am the beginning AND the END

                    2   5 : 7
77
The Prince of Peace

I Am . . .
              First AND last
              TAYLOR   RUSSELL   STONE
ONE WAY   Two NINE   NINE   Three   ONE Five
              2 6   5   5   5   5   2   5 6 5   6 5
                     18   17   22
      LOVE   GOD   LORD
                     57

                    Permute +1-1 :66   The Rock of ISRAEL

ANOTHER TAYLOR   RUSSELL   STONE
      WAY   Two   NINE   NINE Three   ONE   Five
          2 6   6 5   6 5   2 5   6 5 6 5
              19   18   "22"
          STONE   LOVE   LORD

                    59 : 77 The Prince of Peace
          PERMUTE +2-2

              TAYLOR RUSSELL STONE
                  28   25   19 :   72
          5-4, 1944
              9   9   9
      NINE NINE NINE
       24   24   24   :   72
      The INCARNATE God
       15   40   17   :   72
      The King of Creation   :   72

                    52

I Am . . .
First AND Last

TAYLOR R. STONE
2   9   1   5
11   6
17
764 = 17 : GOD
S   T   O   N   E
ONE TWO SIX FIVE FIVE
16   13   16   24   24
93 : 66 : The Rock of ISRAEL
-3+3   15   20   3   28

S/TONE
ONE   18
655
16
5-3-5-3 9441 PERMUTE 944153-53
Immanu-el
Oh, Immanu-el

STONE   LORD   LOVE
93   29162424   29162424
93   93

.